P9-EDR-663

The Horse Opera
and other poems

The Horse Opera
and other poems

BY MAC HAMMOND

Ohio State University Press

FOR ERSKINE McKINLEY

Acknowledgments

"Still Life with Villeins and Iris" was originally published in the "Partisan Review," Vol. XXI, No. 4 (July–August, 1954).

"Our Inherited House" was originally published in the "Sewanee Review," Vol. LXVI, No. 1 (1958).

"Snapshot" and "In Memory of V. R. Lang" were originally published in "Poetry" in June, 1950, and July, 1964, respectively.

"Where the Tall Corn Grows" and "Life Cycle" were originally published in the "Hudson Review," Vol. VI, No. 1 (Spring, 1953).

"Suburban Nocturne," "Charlottesville, Virginia," "Overture II" to "The Horse Opera" (under the title "Some Years after the War"), "Snipe Hunt," and "The Pied Piper" were originally published in "Audit."

"Something for the Children," "Prometheus," "L'Après-midi d'un Faune," and "Advice to the Grand Council" were originally published in "Audience."

"Encore: The Old Prospector" from "The Horse Opera" and "The Forest" were originally published in "Fubbalo."

"Carrion Crow" and "We Went by Car at Night" were originally published in the "i.e., The Cambridge Review," Vol. I, No. 1 (Fall, 1964) and No. 6 (Winter, 1965).

"The Western Gate" was originally published in "Polemic."

"The Horse Opera" was originally published in "Audit/Poetry," Vol. IV, No. 2 (November, 1965).

Contents

Still Life with Villeins and Iris

Once upon a time, there, lived a man all his life.
The wood, the thatch, the stones are washed away,
But underneath the iris stubs and rock, a knife
Or bowl or pot or broken cup could say
What was his daily bread. From the fields

Ralph came home, smelling like a horse or hay,
To swill his soup and want his wife
And laid her down, yes, every night
And went to sleep with bad dreams of the Devil
Riding the Scarlet Whore up steep and down.

Iris grow there now, their purple roots
Reach the nearest damp and, digging, clutch
At dreams of long ago and curl around the midden
Where he ate; and maybe some old bone that walked
Within the underling, chalks the flower white.

Suburban Nocturne

On this level plot of ground, almost a square
Except for the five-foot stretch behind the house
Where hemlock and lilac screen the neighbors,
An Algonquian chief and eight of his tribe,
Exhausted from stalking the scattering deer,
Lay down at dusk beside spent horses
And slept, uneasy, sprawled around a fire.
Perhaps there was one who kept on riding,
Riding, riding the deer, the creeks and ditches,
Who leapt with the deer to a deeper forest
And dark, deadlocked in branches and antlers,
Awoke, astonished, to hunt among the stars.

Our Inherited House

Suppose a god up there in the attic,
Maybe golden, lost among past days,
Some broken thing, not past mending,
That, pieced together, we could praise.

Suppose we found the pieces, arms, a leg,
And fused them to the torso, torso to the head,
And, as we did, the rafters, full of light
Lit up the fears we shatter in our bed.

Suppose the luminous mouth to speak,
Hands raised in a gesture of peace
To call us through the window to the sky—
My love, would we believe our blazing hearts,
Or come back here to the living room and die?

Charlottesville, Virginia

If I fell in the North Rivanna River,
Dropped from a bridge, dying as I fell,
My skin and blood and bones would float
Through Fluvanna County down to the James,
Drift from shore to red-clay shore,
And sweep into Richmond and on by.
Below Richmond I would join the tide
Where hard-shelled crabs click chop-stick claws
And quickly do away with flesh and blood.
Churned in the out-poured turmoil of the James,
My skeleton, joint-free, would scrape a path
Between Old Point Comfort and Willoughby Spit
To be engulfed at last in the large Atlantic flood.
But, before passing on, past Cape Henry, south,
I would take a trip. North at Buckroe Beach
My frame, inched back and forth in the tide,
Would beach and bleach bone-white in the sun.
I could wait for a storm: and, struggling free,
Edge on the mud-packed floor of Chesapeake Bay,
Past the swelling delta of the York,
And stop at the soft expanse of the Potomac.
There, poised between an equal ebb and flow,
My bones would catch in a sunken thicket of trees.
I might lie, tangled in twigs, a year, a century,
Before the tide would wear the trees away
And pull me twenty miles upstream toward the capital.
So close again to vast urbanity, my bones

Might wish to creep on hands and knees
Up to the moonlit, electric city
To perform an ultimate gesture. Absurd idea!
My spindly bones, polished till almost worn away,
Languid in water, with such desire
Would melt, dissolve, diffuse instead
And gush to the deepest mysteries of the sea.

II

The Horse Opera

For Katka

Mon bateau partira demain pour l'Amérique
Et je ne reviendrai jamais
Avec l'argent gagné dans les prairies lyriques. . . .

—Apollinaire

I turn round and round irresolute some-
times for a quarter of an hour, until I decide,
for the thousandth time, that I will walk into
the Southwest or West. Eastward I go only by
force; but Westward I go free.

—Thoreau

Curtain Raiser

Channel 14 in the Key of C

When The Cowboy, done with shooting, off
His horse, off-stage, spent, standing by the kliegs
And cameras, unmasks and smokes his cigarette,
He speaks to all of us. Note the tilt
Of his square-cut jaw, the cleft in his chin,
How the simple bandana half covers his ample
Adam's apple—in spasm at exhale.
Justice is done. His name is Rock
Or Adam Something, but now he will confess
"My name is . . . " any Tom, Telemachus, or Dick
Just like the rest of us.

                      I am not persuaded.
And now, profile, close up, in American English
He explains why this here filtered cigarette
Gives me pleasure.
                Next program.

Too soon the image fades. I linger with him,
Still admire the clean-cut of The Cowboy, his V
Torso, his two side-slung six-shooters.
I am still out West, to find what he is like,
This man, daring to be the father of my country.

13

Prelude

Let me lay the scene: a Western plain:
In all directions, level with the eye, horizon.
At our feet a ditch, half-filled with water,
Around which grows the only green in sight,
Dry tufts of grass, a tangled cactus.
Nothing moves, unless the white clouds overhead
Inch toward the West. The sun, straight up
Beats down. Look! Look to the East, at land's edge,
A dot. I think it is a man comes riding—
It is The Cowboy, lean and tall and handsome!
He swings, easy, from his tooled-leather saddle,
Unstraps a canvas-padded steel canteen,
Bends to the stagnant pool and, with his hand,
Skims the green scum to the side, and drinks,
Bathes his wrists, and, when the pool is still,
Looks at the face he has not seen for days.

Three blocks south, the tires of midnight trucks
Buzz on the concrete strip of Highway 3,
And, through the hemlocks, dark against the fence,
Their headlamps graze the darkness of the lawn.
The whitest peonies are ghosts, and, overhead,
The sycamore weaves gently with the stars.
Shrouded in this scene, I lack all moral sense.
Therefore, The Cowboy rises, mounted, from his grave,
The rosebed heaves and, suddenly, spews up
Skeletons: Poet, Soldier, Sailor, Bigamist.
And then, The Cowboy's gunfire rakes the drying shrubs
And kills the cricket's high-pitched music there.
I hail The Cowboy, try calling him by name:
"Cowboy, dismount!" and, swaggering he comes—
Spurs clanking as he strides the terrace stones—
And, in the lawn chair next to mine, sits down.

A crownéd jay, late yesterday, in the spruce,
Thumped among the darkest inner fronds,
Furtive to hide some awkward piecemeal thing
Borne between his bright blue wing and bill.
The jay, I guess, screamed once, shrilly in a human voice,
And, then, caught up in sudden gusts of storm,
Vanished in the swirling maples of my neighbor's lawn.
After the great blue bird had flown beyond my care,
I found, clutched to the spruce's inner core,
The Sailor's arm. Then, wildwind tossed the tree
And rain, a rain of stunted pine cones pelted down.
I admit: the day before, I found beside the garden hose,
Stretched out behind the coral bells and thyme,
The Cowboy's thigh, and nearby, in the peonies,
Partly shattered on the grass beside the laurel,
The Poet's head. These hulks were not in marble—
Nor was The Soldier's hurt and withering white hand.
Why do they return? I thought these men were dead.
Why do they return! Even this peaceful evening,
Snuffed out below the graceful chaliced rose, I found
The cruel Bigamist's angry black cigar.

Once, yesterday, or maybe yesterday, at dawn,
I sat in the garden, mending The Poet's head,
One ear beyond repair, the other trumpeted,
Mouth dumb; but in his blue and lidless eyes
I heard the hoofbeats of The Cowboy's mare
And, cautious lest my movement summon him,
Rose, mysterious, to shut the garden gate.
The hoofbeats dwindled, I returned, surprised
To find The Cowboy seated in my cast-iron chair,
Slouched and arrogant, fumbling to undo
The blooded bandage in The Poet's hair.
I rustled. Even the words I spoke were dry:
"You are my image; the broken speechless face
You hold within your hands is my face too."

Aria I: The Preacher

Dearly beloved, we are gathered together here,
At Idlewild, under the porch of the westbound ramp,
Our voices raised above the roar of the incoming jets,
To pray for the souls of stars, Hollywood actors
Cooper and Gable, Gary and Clark—they
Rode stallions through the mountains of our dreams;
And, across this silver screen, ride to a last sunset.
To them, American honors: the Stars and Stripes
Shall be their shroud; our anthem, dirge.

Almighty God, though we walk through the Valley
Of Almighty Death, such shadows we shall not see again:
Gable's gambler smile, taking a Chinaman's chance
With Shady Sal, draw poker, stud, and death;
Cooper's lank limbs' slow stride to set a town in order.

In this urn, their ashes, and something of our tears.
Americans, hear this protestant eulogy and benediction.
The Boeing 707, out there, straining to taxi
Across the runway strips, is ready for flight.
An hour from here, over lyrical plains in the West,
I shall scatter their dust with the dust of roses
And say, "I, poet-priest, the right hand of God,
Bequeath these ashes, these roses, to the busted sod."
For I am The Preacher. Out West I bless the town
When The Cowboy, wounded, and the sun go down.

Aria II: The Wagon Master

Lieutenant Hammond, jg, US Naval Reserve,
Retired, a veteran on the old men's list.
I am thirty-six. My papers say I cannot go to war
Unless, unlikely, the President himself shall call
Madmen for defense.

                           And yet, I am The Sailor,
My mind the sea on which, today, I sail
A prairie schooner, WSW, toward that Holy City,
Santa Fe.
                My insanity, it is serene: fascination
To see the color blue, the sea, the sky
And, when most mad, those around me from the Testaments.

I had my training on the *Merrimac;*
I think we sank the *Monitor.*

This madness is divine.

Aria III: The Badman

(For Jack Palance)

Of course I keep two wives, one East, one West,
One for the devil's dance and one for the devil's evil.
Bigamist, Badman, whatever my name,
Black Jack I am, I am Black Jack, the same
Rack of a man my father was, a gun
Quick to unload at anyone, a long brag
Of a boy with a girlish face, hands
Ice, lip acurl, a cruel snarl, a curse
Unstrung from my cradle, a marked
Card, a fancy, dandy Jack-in-the-Box, I
Am always twenty-one, I deal the cards, I
Always win, showdown, one-eyed
Jack dealt from below or from up the sleeve,
A fourletterword scratched on a privy wall,
I make you do the things you do
You want to forget, over and over again.
Gunslinger, I lay them all in the dust
And travel. From Cleveland, now, to Sante Fe,
Motorcycle motor athrob between my legs,
I race to overtake and undertake The Cowboy,
That chaste man, bride for my silver bullets.

Quartet: *The Four of Us Were Quarreling*

The Bigamist said, yes, poetry has its use.
It serves at least two amorous ways,
To help some lover grumbling on his bed
Kill time or save it repeating a memorable phrase.

The Sailor said, yes, poetry has its use.
Those who wander far from birth to death
Have many willing guides but none so sure
As the enduring sound of a deadman's breath.

The Cowboy said, yes, poetry has its use,
As good as a gun it puts a town in order,
Establishes peace in the heart's corral
And drives the heart's bandits over the border.

And I, The Poet, I said, yes, poetry has its use.
And I will make it. I will make it plain,
Aspiring to music. Like the poet William Yeats
I will make it from my pleasure and my pain.

Aria IV: The Barkeep

Drunk as I am, I still walk the solid line
Strung out for me a hundred years ago
When Jakob Hamman, a faithless German Jew,
Shot through the head, one side of Beacon Hill,
The rebel guard who, a year before, had lacerated him.
I raise three fingers of Old Grandad to my greatgrandfather
And his revenge. He was small and wiry,
A tangle of string, and unwound west in Ohio.

His only son, John Brown, grew up to be obsessed
By murder. When he was six, my father's father watched
A drunken man cave in, with a flatiron, the head of another.
At twenty-six he destroyed a saloon with a roaring chair
And began the public murder of The Demon Rum.
John Brown Hammond fought to his death John Barleycorn,
And old, defeated, blind like Homer, wrote
The Rise and Fall of Prohibition and the Way Back.

The way back—so many dead soldiers, so much blood.

At twenty-six, when John B. was Chief of Police,
Dumping gallons of bootlegged booze in the Des Moines,
My father, his only son, easy-speaking, took to drink.
For all I cared, he could have murdered me.

But, now my only son is born, here again in Ohio,
I raise three fingers of Old Grandad to my father,
Sober and flat on his back with a cancerous mouth,
And forgive him.

Now free of all that
I go further west, a hundred years ago, to Santa Fe,
To keep the bar, to serve one shot, to The Cowboy.
Am I the Jack of Diamonds? I am the Jack of Hearts.

Aria V: The Girl from the East

Sick of my cubbyhole on Beacon Hill, of Boston and TV,
I rifle an antique chest-of-drawers for clothes,
Put on a long-curl wig, a whalebone skirt, a bonnet,
And prim, proper, pink-fringed sunshade up,
Fly away, in stages, toward the buffalo.
I arrive, made-up, a schoolmarm, a Quaker,
The naïve Girl-from-the-East in the West.
My disguise is perfect. Even the U.S. Marshal
Does not suspect—nor the shuffling Hotel Clerk
Who gives me a room, with quilt and stove and bath
Overlooking The Saloon. Yes, I told them,
All my brothers died in the war. A private eye,
And still demure, I sign the register *Louise*.

Aria VI: The Indian Chief

(For Cora Dubois)

*Ghosts go wandering through a
monotonous apocalypse in search
of lost friendship with nature
and human beings.*
—Camus

Betrayed, betraying, I
Walked the lands of my forefathers, loose
And angry, looking for a friend.
White men failed me, even the President
Of these United States, until I
Stood, alone, atop this mesa,
Spread out below me all these canyons
Whose

       bends
       breaks
       rush of currents
       rapids
       gorges
       turns
       sharp
       and
       grand

I knew by heart.

Aria VII: The Harvard Man

I am a lucky number (after thirteen years
In the graduate school); *Philosophiae Doctor*
Making 65 (in '62) on the Western Reserve.

Can't ride this horse, can't shoot this gun
(It's the best horse, it's the best gun);
I only look the part. A dude, a dud
(I bought my duds at Brooks;
My saddlebags are full of books)
And parenthetical, pathetic, when The Badman
Draws (highhand) and The Cowboy fires,
I cringe, I crowd to the outhouse floor
(The townsfolk laugh—"What is knowledge for?")
I am over-learned, I know I know
(And knowing how to write, I write this down):
I must be there (aside) in Sante Fe
When The Badman draws and The Cowboy
Fires, for, without me, who could think?
(And the old world could never meet the new).

Aria VIII: The Sodbuster

I neglect my father's grave.
Another winter and the snow
Drifts against the stone
I have not set.

Aria IX: The Cowboy

I wish I was The Cowboy.
I wish I were Cocteau.
I wish I were Proust.
I wish my chickens
Would come home to roost.
I wish I had a gun.
I wish I were my son.

I wish I may
I wish I might
Be the movie star
I see tonight.

Aria X: The Rebel Soldier

I am utterly defeated.
The Stars and Bars shall never rise again.
I am a slave to my own desires.

Santa Fe
Is a hundred years
Away.

Ladies and Gentlemen,
The program is over.
I have but one word
More
To say: LOVE

Encore: The Old Prospector

Once more I bring the pickaxe down
Amid the rubble of this mountainside.
Years have passed and I, alone,
No longer search to find what you call
Gold. Gold is not worth looking for.
I say I struck it rich in stones.

III

In Memory of V. R. Lang (1924–1956)

I wore this very dress
The night that Virgil died.

I was there and I remember the brown brocade
With pearls like tears gleaming on the bodice.
We lounged at court, at ease, on lavender cushions,
Toasting Augustus, when Maecenas brought the news.
I remember you held his wrinkled ringless hands,
Gazing deep for comfort in his ancient eyes,
Avoiding relevant words. He looked like Death.
You rose to depart, draped like an autumn goddess,
The jewel I gave you burning at your throat,
And fainted. I caught you as you drifted down.
But, you were no friend to Virgil, wrote him no poems.
The hurt was deeper. Once we stood in the Forum
And stared at a pompous hearse. Your beautiful eyes,
Full of the tears of the ages, said everything dies.

Prometheus

There was nothing in the paper bag but fire
Which I, unmoved, removed for other men
Moving away and away and toward the bag
As though under water rather than air.
They seemed indifferent but I could see
Excitement, once in a while, in their eyes,
When, especially bright and clear, flames
Passed from my cold hands to theirs.

L'Après-midi d'un Faune

Once upon an ordinary afternoon
I walked as usual the forest out of town
And came expectedly upon the clump of pine
Where Pithys died and Echo disappeared.
Something in my nature wept. I smiled
Remembering they did not love me;
That they fled in what is now called panic;
That Pithys, her face still distinct
On the ravenous trunk of the tree,
Cursed my divinity and begged me go;
That Echo's last word was *Narcissus*.

For the first time it seemed possible:
Three thousand years ago they died;
I was no longer sure which tree was *the* tree
And from blue mountains across the lake
Echo no longer answered my taunts.

Admiring my face in the beautiful lake
I thought *How clever you are; no one knows*
What you conceal with shoes and trousers
And, frolicking, kicked them off, airing
My thighs and shaggy cloven feet. Foolish!
The woods, of course, was full of women
Who race and give me no rest.

The Prodigal Son

My little drunken father, speak the words
Again that burned your sons. I will
Listen now with burnished ears and eyes
Golden with experience. Your love
Is moving now your touch is gone.
How far and such a road I traveled (sigh).
I come back almost too late to find you dead.
My feet! My feet, how many steps
On the jewels of the world and clean
Yet. My hands? You ask to see my hands?
You know, as well as I, they were not used.
But I have turned and turned and, coming home,
Have you at a distance in my arms.

Atlantis II

Here in Atlantis the slopes I walk
Look like the streets on Beacon Hill:
Salt encrusts on everything like snow;
The sea I breathe is thick blue air;
And fish, up there, are aeroplanes.
This green-gold dome adrift, was once the Capitol;
That ivory archway where I went to church;
That rubble, where I first made love,
A shattered column in the thoroughfare.
Phosphorescent people pass, pale
Irishmen perhaps, engulfed. And I
Construct these verses while we drown!

Children of the Mandrake

We were full of gloom the moment we drew breath.
Because our blood was bad, our eyes were red.
The earth was howling for us, and we fled.

Once upon a Time There Was a Man

Once upon a time there was, there was a man
Who lived inside me wearing this cold armour,
The kind of knight of whom the ladies could be proud
And send with favours through unlikely forests
To fight infidels and other knights and ordinary dragons.
Once upon a time he galloped over deep green moats
On bridges princes had let down in friendship
And sat at board the honoured guest of kings
Talking like a man who knew the world by heart.
In every list he fought, the trumpets on the parapets,
The drums, declared his mastery, the art of arms;
His horse, the household word of every villager,
Was silver-shod and, some said, winged.
Once upon a time, expecting no adventure
In the forest everybody knows, at midnight,
He saw a mountain rise beneath the moon.
An incredible beast? With an eye of fire?
He silently dismounted, drew his famous sword
And hid behind the heavy trees and shrubs to see
If what he thought he saw was real. He fled
And the giant eye of the moon pursues him still.

Advice to the Grand Council

In another Babylonia the kings
Gave land away. Rents and fields
Were free and we were all perfect,
Gentlemen. No one complained, the city
Glittered with gold and in our grand attire
We strolled arm in arm on and on.

Foreign dukes of course made war.
Under siege we flooded suburbs
But in our fear, fell from one another.
My son stole a diamond I tucked away
And swore to the police I housed a spy;
But it was years before, I had a duke to dinner.

We kept no government and, grown soft,
Those who took up arms we called divine;
Ragged, undrilled, they were our law:
Speakers muted, pacifics hanged—
I saw a man gut another for his skin—
All illuminated scrolls were burned.

When food gave out and plague
Crawled from sewers to the reservoir
I think some ate each other;
The dukes refused a self-contaminated city,
Commissioned slaves cleared rubbish and the bones.

Now we have rebuilt a marble city
And joined by invitation many federations.
But will we walk as we used to do?
Look at our sons. My son in school
Hears words ages of humanity inspire
But is self-consumed and has, although desire,
No hope for a golden age like ours.

First Days at Barmaco Station

Nothing to drink in this desert for days.
Black girls bring me rose-colored waters.
They wrap cool ribbons around my head.
The food is a bane, a pain, a poison.
I lie for hours curled on my bed.
I pack and unpack my box and my trunk.
The northbound train carries others away.

Evenings, I walk with the village daughters.
These natives mean nothing to me—their ways
Are strange and sober. I would be drunk!

IV

On Seeing the Elgin Marbles for the First Time

(After Rilke)

You cannot gaze into his vanished face
Which, legends say, was blinding like the sun;
But at his struggling torso you can trace
Light, bright enough to stun.

His breast curve like a chain of stars
Gleams toward his broken lifting thighs
And dazzles in those hollow middle scars
Where so much lived no longer lies.

If you saw that marble radiance die
Or lessen, you would pass him by
Like other shattered demigods of Greece

But, rising, ruined, fallen from his frieze,
He gathers brilliance in his strife
And shines through you. You must remake your life.

Darwiniana

Carnivorous giraffes broke out in spots
To camouflage themselves from death
And, stretching up like trees to trees,
Took their fullest nourishment from these.

Winged reptiles, fleeing north, toward the ice,
Lost the art of being warm and died;
While timid elephants compressed their necks
And closed in hide their enormous intellects.

Transparent birds with frantic arms like twigs
Burst into feather, becoming beautiful,
And stupid monkeys, frightened until then,
Talked and walked together and were men.

Life Cycle

Dropped on velvet leaves
The stuff you swallow down
Impetuously weaves
Too long a ragged gown,
Moth, Moth, forming eye.

With your many legs and feet
Eating up and down
Your forest street
You'll grow a better gown,
Moth, Moth, glutted eye.

The careful house you spin
Will silken all your dress;
Yourself all builded in,
Now beautiless,
Moth, fading eye. Now

Your curléd horns are black
And rainbows overflow
Your velvet back;
Your lust is go, go,
Moth, glittering eye.

Whirling round in flame
With love's exhaustible excess

You end your dressing game
In tatteredness,
Moth, Moth, vanishing eye.

But your pale embalméd wings
Caught, pinned, and set,
As this poem sings
Are fluttering yet,
Moth, Moth, polished eye.

The Only Christian Thing to Do

The last man to decide was a scholar,
A small man from a small town in Holland.
He came of his own free will and signed
What everyone else had signed, a paper
Where was agreed to abolish the premise of God.
He was the last man to accept the Absurd:
That the future was dead as dead men
And all lived or would live in the present.
But, that night, when everyone went to bed,
Content that tomorrow was absurd as today,
A runaway priest and two acolytes, adolescents,
Took passage on the first trip to the moon.
At two fifteen ante meridiem they landed
Perfectly safe. They constructed a lunar cathedral.
Two twelve-year-old boys and an English priest
Set a golden bell in a silica steeple
And, dying of thirst and the terrible weather,
Marked out two billion sun-scorched graves
For about two billion indifferent people.

Carrion Crow

Pink dogwood peppered the treescape pink.

Under branches I walked like a natural thing,
Free from books, from books into the air,
When up in an oak, a crow with carrion
Slowed my thought and stride again to philosopher's gait.
I watched the vulture nibble and tear
And he knew it. Heavy with mouse or mole
I saw him lumber from limb to limb
With the slow-motion flop of his wings
And slouch behind trunks of cedar and ash.
I clapped, he dropped, he flew, I ran, he soared
Up, up out of sight and left me
Heaving for breath at the edge of an endless plain,
Flat and unfriendly. Did he go up or out?
Was this the rumored edge of the earth?
I clung with one hand to a stump,
While still out of sight and below me,
A black monster, circling, circling,
Craved and abided lost flesh.

Rome, 1955

Around the broken Forum Rome survives the war;
Around the Colosseum lions and lambrettas roar.

Naples, 1955

I took my wilderness along, up the funicular,
And stood at the city's cliff, Naples, the bay,
And the islands composed in levels below.
I wandered there. The palace I had come to see
Was dull or locked or used now by the army.
Without a guide I dumbly saw that city,
Church by church, the sloping streets, the vista.
Perhaps because Vesuvius rose in the distance
I thought of Jesus, hungry on a mountain,
Surveying all the kingdoms of the world.

A Tree in the Distance and Getting There

That tree in the prospect among trees,
That single oak, clumped amid birch,
Beyond this field of autumn corn
Towers highest, towers above top tassels
And lures us, beckons us on
Past this thick cattail slough.
Come, we walk heavy through brambles,
Briars, burrs, jimson, and milkweed
On this slope, steep to the oak tree.
Look up, through, see the sky
Ripe with acorns, leaves and twigs,
Old twigs, ready to fall
And scatter down toward the slough.

Where the Tall Corn Grows

Over drumlands all the trees of Iowa green
Made me wish the glaciers had not melted
On Missouri's head, but pushed southward
Past even Tennessee to Texas' gulf
And left its black silt to salt the continent
And grow all verdure that green.

In Iowa leaves higgle for color and highness
And fall from peers of summer's green:
So red is the sumac on the copper-coated oak
The trees, the trees in a seasonal trish-trash
Are God's covenant on terrestial destruction
But for its blues, its arch, and highness.

In winter how they so naked stand
And clip and chip about their sometime green
And point their sapless lumber in a limber highness:
As a child I used to act their human numbness
And feeling like trees over and over
Would chatter and so, naked stand.

In spring by one and one leaves reappear
In pushes of royal green green
And that same child I was would beg their highness
To bend a fragile crown down where I stand

And anoint me with an Iowa's April rain.
Sceptered now with memory, I reappear,

Hoisting up a trunk, along the limbs
To twigs, to leaves, undone with green,
And see from an Iowa tree's green highness
Iowa, her endless drumlands, this year's stand
Of grain, her Indian maize plainly appear,
And free my homely limbs.

The Ferret

My father standing with me by a woodshed spoke:
There are a million rabbits in that cord of wood.
With a weathered stick of lathe he pointed to a wedge
Where between the logs our old black spaniel
On her belly slipped in and chased them out
Like a ferret, said my father, *like a ferret.*
I took then the figures of his speech for fact
And even to this day when I recall my father
I see the woodshed where he stood like a magician,
The silver stick of lathe, the stack of wood, the wedge
With rabbits and rabbits and a ferret coming out.

Catching a Crab on Wednesday

My father was dying. Only the boat,
The boat we chartered for the annual
Picnic, was calm in smooth water.
Only ripples edged from our ship.
We were the center of the pool, the eye
Of a hurricane, wind that undid
The structures over the years others
Had built. And I was calm.
Only this, this only I can tell,
Only the agile oars, as the saying is,
Were, well-oiled, stuck in the locks.

The Pacific

Your name is Pacific, but you snarl
Among these rocks, amorphous monster.
Hermaphrodite, the winds enrage
Your sexless sleep, and what you dream
Is thrust and broken on the shore:
There lies a plume that fanned
Some Pharaoh three thousand years ago . . .
A wave rolls in and drops the vestments
Of a Roman Jew, and, now, upon the beach
I see the driftwood of the ages, tangled,
Torn and polished, snagged in the seaside stones:
Anglo-Saxon amulets, a Norman tower,
Elizabeth's own ruffled dress of state,
Catgut from the lyre of Orpheus,
The arm of my cousin, Carl, destroyed last year in a jet . . .

VI

We Went by Car at Night

So soon, and the heartbreak quest is over?
Did we really see that city, spend the night
Carousing in the ruins, drunk till dawn
On green, liquid, waving, eddied air?
Surely a dream. Did I really take you there
And long enough to ease your tongue
On that soft polyphonic language?

I remember we drove down mountains to the sea,
Six aching miles beyond the beach, and plunged
Down for hours. In the closing dark we saw
Nothing, until, yet far below, a flashing light
Took on shape, and, turning, we knew we were there
At Atlantis, the oldest city of the sea.

The Forest

When, days later, we reached the end of the path
And lay at last among voluptuous leaves,
We swore we never should see days go by so fast again.
By day our words were marked by time, but all night long
The language that we spoke was, like the brightest star,
Fixed, it seems, forever, in one place.
Did you find out alone the high road back?
I know you sleep among the rows of empty houses now,
While I lie here, still, tangled in these leaves.

The Love Nest

That was surely a dream: You were falling
And I, unable to scream, crouched on a ledge,
My huge right hand, punctured and deflating,
Fumbling a hold in sand, my six legs
Dangling a thread, spun out of my groin,
Toward your bed, there, in the web below.
And, then, your wings, at last, unlocked;
You flew, in rings, around my hissing head.
My skin turned green, and, ugly, I sought cover
And still will not be seen. Why did you raid my nest
And vanish forever? I kept there nothing, nothing,
Which now, aflame, is loose, alone, in the air.

Aubade

In your dark hair I wonder what dreams
And where does your knowledge lie. Asleep
Your face takes on the light and seems
Stone.

Is such tender love and furious I know
This morning dead in you or will you rise
Fully adorned with yesterday
With all my love signaled in your eyes?

Snapshot

Your beauty was candid and angular
And asked for development. Thief
I posed a picture not singular
And now album my grief.

The eye's little photograph
Wets your negative, see how
All past loves lie
Exposed now.

Snipe Hunt

The snipe is a rare bird the heart of which
    was once
        the delight of kings.

The snipe is almost blind and runs at night
    in fields
        toward
            light.

The snipe has no wings, no tail.
    The snipe
        never
            sings.

To catch a snipe, hold a mirror
    reflecting light
        from a pale
            moon.

Silent, no sound, hold the mirror
    above a bag
        held open
            to the ground.

The snipe will run to you and you
    will hold
        the snipe
            trembling in your hand.

You know how to snare love,
Then, you can snare this bird.

Calmly, Calmly Night Came On

Calmly, calmly night came on
Through solid walls of stone on stone
But from the streets the ghosts were gone
Who wreathed together flesh and bone.

Through solid walls of steel and stone
I drove a pale white deathless horse
And stopped at strangers I had known
To beg a living body's force.

And was denied. My reinless horse
Rode, he raced from dawn to dawn
Through walls that once had been my course,
Through streets from which my ghost was gone.

Atlantis III

If I could find what I am looking for,
The first thing I would do would be to raise
Atlantis, and we would go there, two by two.

If I could find what I am looking for,
Within me, I would, for you, rewrite the world
And we would live there, careless who

We were some days ago or will become.
I would, as now, as yesterday, forever then,
Refuse the message of the mortal stars,
And (keep me close) undo what time will do.

VII

Intaglio with Birds

From Cherry Street, the mainway of my capital,
I walked across the tracks and out of town,
Leagued with goldfinches for the afternoon,
And, if brown thrushes were my heart's desire,
I said it simply so, brown thrushes are my heart's desire,
Nested in the bitterweed and bridal wreath.

Here I Go Again

As though it were afraid of that dark journey,
Before I write a poem my mind is static,
Locked in the confines of this disordered house,
All attention fixed on some stupidity,
A bread crumb on the floor, a shuffled garment,
As though it thought by thought to keep the body still,
The body swayed and drifting from its will
Through the very object of regard.
My mind stops, as though it could forget
A knowledge and a love lost somewhere in the past
And wait without them for an easy death.

Something for the Children

The snowman I made, I made
With the careful ease of a sculptor
Accustomed to ironwood and rock.
Children were not delighted
Seeing his anthracite eyes,
His bituminous ears and mouth
Because they knew, they knew
If a passionate sun came out
And everything else was melting,
Their igloo forts and angels,
And hunks of his packed-up body
Were perspiring and trickling away—
His face, hard on the ground
And in pieces, would during and after
And always coldly endure.

The Innocent Bystander

(A Letter to Myself)

You were talking about the music of poetry
When we met last. Reading Donne tonight
I looked up from the page. The quiet continued.
I spoke your name and a poem was destroyed.
That one word amid silence touched the air,
Made me put away poems and speak it again.
The timbre was magnificent and the tone
Suggested I would always be alone.

But you were right on the weakness of Image.
I figured once a short trip to Byzantium
To engulf my suffering, but now I find
I would have to go there. I must master
My mind and weep, as usual, in Cambridge.

We agreed once, remember, that poetry
Was nothing and we would live lavishly,
Go south without it. Remember what we said
About the sensuous apprehension of thought,
That our sensibility was all dissociate?
And how we laughed when we read aloud:

"The blushful Hippocrene with beaded bubbles"
And lifted pure sparkling burgundy
To your "purple stainéd" mouth?

I forget how we rejected mimesis exactly;
Only Sartre's "illusion of immanence" remains.
We decided, finally, poetry was not life
But surreality in the imagination.
I wish you had been here when I discovered
The surreal equals the stupid subconscious;
It was a blue day to find what was beautiful
Were unalterable compulsions. I should add
I still think poetry is in the brains,

But poetry is Form. Not of course symmetry:
The right side of the lines may be crooked
And the rhyme and the meter jangle and jig,
But the words, ah, the words form enormous,
Although the black that contains them
Is not very big. *I think I have thought
I thought*, which at first appears nonsense,
But if you think as I thought you will see.

A word of caution. My theory is incomplete:
There is no critique to establish Quality.
I leave it to you to distinguish the Good
From the True and the Beautiful or whatever
You call it. P.S. Please stop writing
And reading those pucker-mouth poems;
Since it is Form you are after, let it be free,
Moved into relations more lovely than ours
Ought to be. Please write yours truly.

The Western Gate

Here I am, Primavera, come to Cleveland.
It is the fall of the year. Leaves are turning red
And nothing in this city seems to resemble
A poem. Can Cleveland be a muse? I have sung
In other cities, living and dead, of the living and dead:
Venezia sinking into the sea and Herculaneum
Inspired my finest elegies; the streets of Napoli,
That joyous ode. But Cleveland? Here I am, Primavera,
Teaching others how to write, when, certainly,
Primavera, I should have followed you abroad
To learn more secrets from your painless art.
Now, five thousand miles away, I wonder
If the Terminal Tower, Ninth Street, or the Lake Erie
Will ever seem more than tower, street, and lake.
But one day, in Wade Park, a single fountain may recall
All the fountains of Trevi; or, some afternoon,
A lecture on poetry done, as I walk away
To Piccola Italia and home, a Cleveland elm,
Spraying up like a fountain, may recall
The solitary elms that stood forlorn
In the corners of corn fields, farther west,
In Iowa, where, one spring, my peregrine bones were born.

The Pied Piper

The tune I played was only music;
Only the tone of my flute was magic,
Was what the children of that tropic,
That winter, heard and found so tragic.